Rocks and Soils

By the end of this book you will know more about:

- Different kinds of rocks.

- Where rocks come from and what they are used for.

- How soil is formed.

- The differences between soils.

You will:

- Plan a fair test investigation.

- Use Fact Files, books, CD-ROMs and the Internet for research.

You can use rocks for many different purposes.

Task 1 | *Rocks and soils in the kitchen*

Our lives depend upon rocks and soils. We need them to grow our food, build our houses and to make many important things. Even the planet we live on is mainly rocks and soils.

Look at this kitchen. Which things are made from rocks and soils?

Mark them on Task Sheet 1. The Fact File will help you.

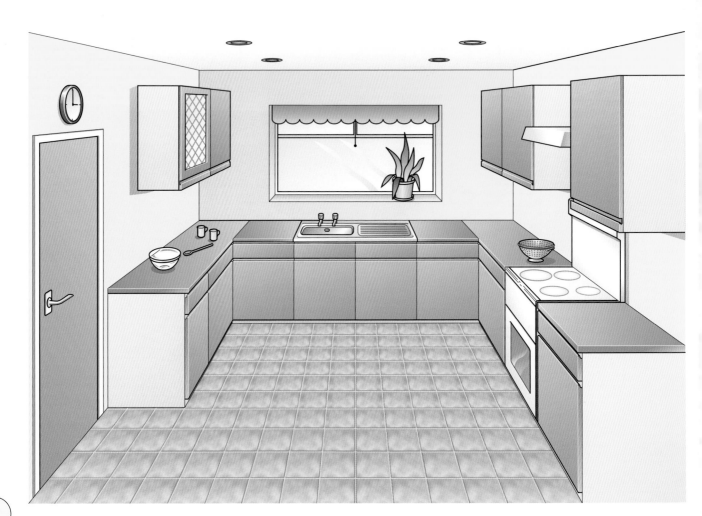

A house built on rock

Fact File

Made from Rock

- Glass is made from special sand and limestone, heated together.

- Metals are found in rocks called ores.

- Plastics are made from oil, which is formed deep under the ground.

- Tiles and bricks are made from clay.

- Pottery is made from clay.

- Many modern clocks contain quartz rock.

You can sort rocks by how they look.
Observe and compare rocks.

How are they different?

Rocks come in many different colours and shapes. Some are heavier than others and some feel different to others.

- Look at your two rocks closely.
- How are they alike?
- How are they different?
- Write the differences on Task Sheet 2.

YOU NEED:

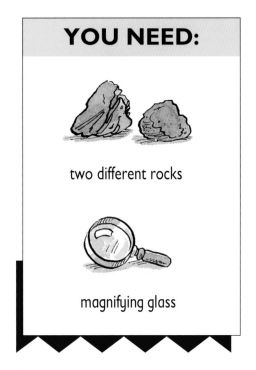

two different rocks

magnifying glass

My first rock	My second rock
heavy sharp edges shiny black	quite light

- Now use the magnifying glass to look closely at the rocks.
  Are they made up of separate bits?
  Are they all one material?

- Wet your rocks with a few drops of water.
  Look again through the magnifying glass.
  What can you see now?

- Draw what you see.
  The tiny pieces can be called **particles**.

Piece of rock showing particles

Task 3 — Make a no-bake rock cake

1 Melt the chocolate and butter over a low heat. Stir a few times.

⚠ *Do not approach a cooker or hot pan without an adult.*

2 Mix in the broken biscuits, the fruit and marshmallows and stir well to coat everything in chocolate.

3 Spoon the mixture onto kitchen foil. Mould your cakes into rock shapes.

4 Chill your cakes in a fridge until hard.

Like many rocks, your cakes will be made up of lots of small particles, all bound together. Slice the cake and look at the particles. Can you identify them?

YOU NEED:

250 g plain chocolate

250 g fruit and nut, fruit and biscuit or fruit chocolate bar

200 g broken digestive biscuits

50 g butter or margarine

50 g small digestive biscuits

50 g small marshmallows or chopped large ones

50 g raisins

50 g cherries

50 g chopped dates or figs

Find differences between rocks by testing.

Scientific Enquiry

How hard?
....

⚠️ *Be careful not to get bits of rock in your eyes.*

✴️ Some rocks are hard and some are soft.
What happens if you rub hard and soft rocks
together?

✴️ Rub two of your rocks together. Which is
the harder rock? How do you know?

✴️ Take your harder rock and challenge
another rock to a rubbing contest.
Which is harder?

✴️ Test the hardness of all your rocks and put
them in order across the table, from hardest
to softest.

YOU NEED:

collection of different rocks

Words to learn
and use:
clay
limestone
ore
particles
quartz

SUMO ROCK
RUBBING CONTEST

Scratch test

You can scratch some rocks with something as soft as your thumb nail.
You need something harder like a coin to scratch some rocks.
You need a steel nail to scratch a few rocks.

- Complete Task Sheet 3.

- *Take care with sharp points.*

- Put the rocks in order of hardness using your thumb nail, a coin and a steel nail.

- Have you any rocks that you can't scratch with nail, coin or steel nail?

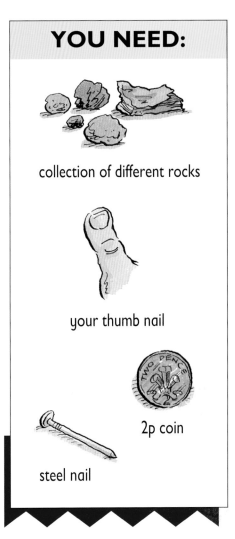

YOU NEED:

collection of different rocks

your thumb nail

2p coin

steel nail

Diamonds

The hardest rocks of all are diamonds. But they are made from the same material as pencil leads and charcoal which are quite soft. It's a bit like ice and water. They are made of the same stuff, and yet ice is harder than water. Inside a diamond, the material, called carbon, forms a strong skeleton. The carbon skeleton inside pencil lead is not as strong.

Different rocks suit different jobs.

House building

A modern house is made from:

8000 house bricks

2250 breeze blocks

10 cubic metres of cement

23 tonnes of sand

800 roof tiles

260 metres of wood

1000 gallons of water

450 metres of electric cable

280 metres of copper piping

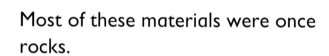

Most of these materials were once rocks.

- **Bricks**, **tiles** and **chimney pots** are made from clay.
- **Cement** is made from clay and rock.
- Lightweight **breeze blocks** are made from cinders, sand and cement.
- **Mortar** - which sticks bricks together - is made from lime, sand, cement and water.
- **Glass** and glass fibre are made with sand and limestone.
- Toilets, basins and some baths can be made from **porcelain**, which is made from clay.

Look at this house. On Task Sheet 4, label all
the parts of the house that are made from
rocks and soils.

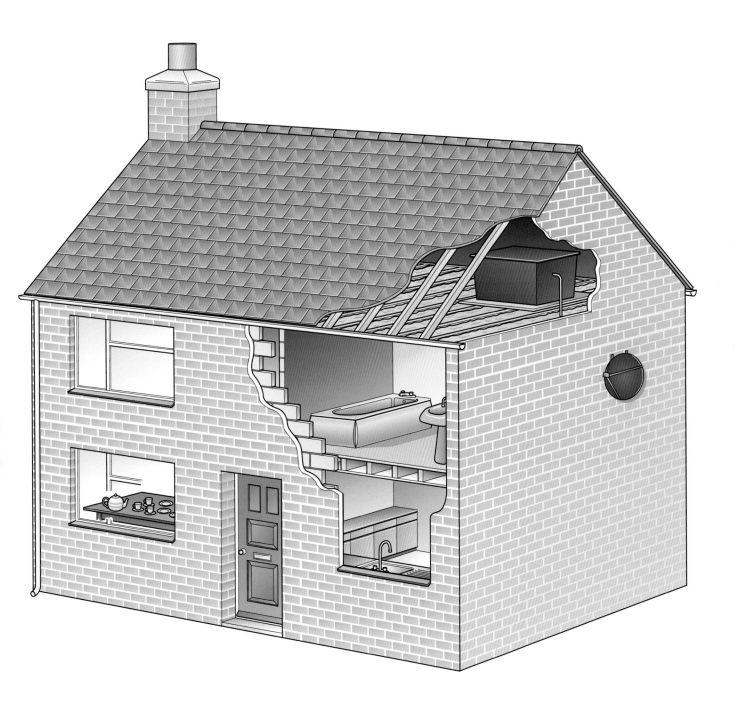

Use CD-ROMs, the Internet and magazines
to research house building materials.

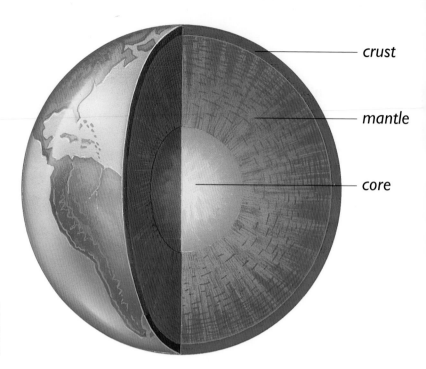

crust

mantle

core

Inside Earth

On solid ground

The planet Earth is a bit like a giant hard-boiled egg. The hard yolk is like Earth's **core**, which is incredibly hot and made of solid iron. The white of the egg is like Earth's **mantle**, which surrounds the core. The mantle is very hot and more like a liquid. It sometimes breaks through the Earth's surface as a volcano. Earth's shell is called the **crust**. It is cold and hard and made of solid rock.

Wherever you stand on the Earth - even if you are on a ship in the middle of the sea - there is rock somewhere beneath you. You are on solid ground.

Just a minute. The school field isn't rock. Nor is the park - or the garden. That's because the rock is covered with a layer of earth or soil. If you dig down through this soil, you will find rock under it – everywhere.

Your profile is the shape of your face, seen from the side. Run your finger down your face, from your hair, down your nose, across your mouth to your chin and neck. This is your profile.

Soil has a profile, too. You can look at it from the side.

If there are some holes being dug nearby, you might be able to visit them as a class or a group. Stand somewhere safe. Look into the hole and study the soil profile.

It is dangerous to go onto building sites and near road works on your own.

Draw or photograph the soil profile.
Look for:

1 **Topsoil** Dark, rich, full of rotting plants.
2 **Subsoil** Different in colour to the topsoil. Tightly packed soil.
3 **Rocky soil** A layer of rock that is breaking down to become soil.
4 **Bedrock** The rock beneath the soil.

Complete Task Sheet 5.

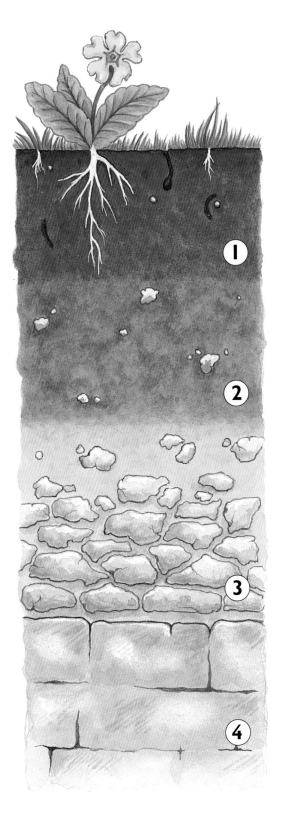

A soil profile

Different types of rock make different types of soil.

Where does soil come from?

The story of Roger Rock

Roger Rock was hard. People broke hammers and spades on his hard, rocky shape. He was proud of being unbreakable. But he was getting worried. Strange things were happening to him. He seemed to be getting smaller.

When the Sun shone on him in the day, he swelled up. When he was cold at night, he shrank away. And all this swelling and shrinking was breaking bits off him.

In the middle of winter, his cracks filled with water. The water froze, and the ice began to push at him. Crack! The ice split him open.

The river that swept past him banged rocks against him, knocking off chips of rock.

Roger Rock crumbled to stone. The stones were rubbed and banged together by the river. They became smaller, turned to gravel, then grains of sand, then a fine powder.

The powder mixed with bits of rotting plants that had bacteria and tiny fungi living on them. It mixed with air and water. Roger Rock looked around. He noticed the changes. He had the wrong name.

"I'm Simon Soil!" he said.

I'm Simon Soil

⚹ Draw your own story of Roger Rock.

⚹ Use the Internet to find out more about soils.

Different rocks, different soils

Not all soil is the same. Different rocks make different types of soil. You can see the differences clearly if you compare what happens to two different soils in water.

✳ Put your soils in the containers.
Add water to each.
Shake or stir them gently.
Leave them overnight to settle.

✳ Draw the differences between the two soils.

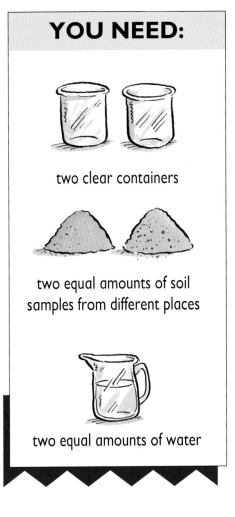

YOU NEED:

two clear containers

two equal amounts of soil samples from different places

two equal amounts of water

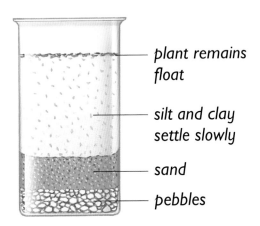

plant remains float

silt and clay settle slowly

sand

pebbles

I This soil is suitable for making bricks.

2 This soil is more suitable for making tiles.

3 This soil is more suitable for making pottery.

Making bricks

In some countries, people test the soil to see how to best use it. They shake it with water and let it settle.

1 If it is a sandy soil - three-quarters sand to a quarter clay - then it is good for making bricks.

2 If it is half clay and half sand, then it is good for making tiles.

3 If it is a clay soil - three-quarters clay to a quarter sand - then it will make good pottery.

 clay

 sand

⭐ Observe differences between soils and make comparisons.

 Task 10 Soil sausages

You can explore the differences between soils by seeing how well you can shape them.

✳ Wet your soil sample.

✳ Wearing waterproof gloves, see if you can roll your soil into a sausage.
If you can, see if it will bend round into a horseshoe, or even a ring.

The more sand soil has in it, the harder it is to roll.
The more clay, the easier it is to shape.

✳ Record your results in a table:

Where my soil sample came from	The shape I could make with it

Sand

Clay

You can separate particles of different sizes by sieving.

A problem at the builder's yard

 6

There has been a mishap in the builder's yard. Different sizes of stones have got mixed up.

Sally has got to sort out the mess!
She has got lots of sieves, but she doesn't know which ones to use.

⭐ Use a ruler to measure the stones and sieves on Task Sheet 6.
Copy and complete this table.

Sieve	What will fall through it?
A	Everything
B	
C	
D	
E	

⭐ Write this heading:

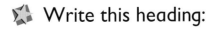

Helping Sally sort it out

⭐ Write instructions for Sally.
Which sieves should she use?
In which order should she use them?

Finding out about soil

Soil is a material. There are different kinds of soil and each kind has its own special properties.

Sandy soil, like its name suggests, contains sand. There are large gaps between the bits of soil. Water drains through very quickly so sandy soils are often dry and light.

Loam soil is not too heavy or too light. Water does not drain through too quickly or too slowly.

Clay soil is heavy and sticky. It is made from fine particles (bits) of clay. The particles do not have much space between them. Water does not drain through easily.

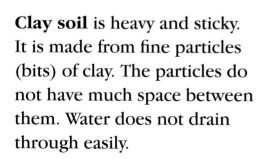

Measure amounts of liquids and time.
Spot an unfair test.

 Task 12

Which soil drains the fastest?

 7,8

- ⚠ *Use plastic gloves when handling soil.*

- ✻ Choose three different kinds of soil.

- ✻ Plan and carry out an investigation to find out which soil drains the fastest.

- ✻ What things will you measure?

- ✻ How will you make sure your test is fair?

- ✻ How much water did you add? How much water drains through each soil?

- ✻ Use Task Sheets 7 and 8 to help you.

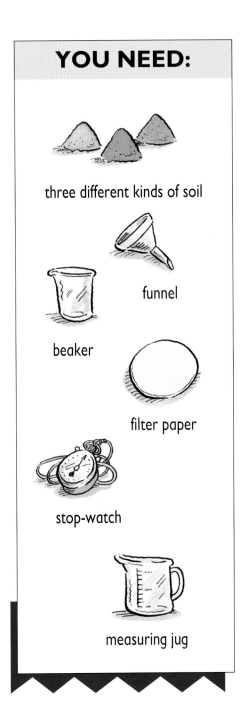

YOU NEED:

three different kinds of soil

funnel

beaker

filter paper

stop-watch

measuring jug

Words to learn and use:
breeze block
carbon
cement
charcoal
concrete
mortar

Plan a fair test.
Explain your results.

Scientific Enquiry

Hannah's garden

Hannah's front garden looked lovely. But her back garden was always covered with water.

"The soil at the front is different to the soil at the back," said Norman the neighbour. "You test it. You'll see."

Norman was always full of smart ideas. This time he just might be right.

Hannah took a pot of soil from the front garden. She wrote 'Front' on it.

She took a pot of soil from the back garden. She wrote 'Back' on it.

She took them into her kitchen.

"How am I going to test these?" she thought.

It was time for Hannah to find out:

1 How much water stayed in each soil.
2 How much water ran through each soil.
3 How quickly the water ran through each soil.

Then she needed to know:

What could she do to the soil to make the water run through it more quickly?
How could she make it drain better?

Hannah collected:

- Two funnels
- A set of scales
- A jug of water
- A seconds timer
- A measuring jug
- Some plastic gloves for handling the soil.

Now what should she do?

Hannah's test

Hannah tested her soils.

She put her results in a table.

It looked like this.

	FRONT GARDEN SOIL	BACK GARDEN SOIL
How does it feel?	Rough, gritty	Smooth, sticky
How does it shape?	Quite well - makes into sausages	Really well - makes into doughnuts with holes
How much water did I add to it?	250 mL	250 mL
How much water drained through	200 mL	120 mL
How long did it take until the water stopped draining?	3 minutes	7 minutes

Which soil let most water through?

Which soil took the longest to drain?

"Well?" said Norman, "what did you find out?"

"The soil in my front garden drains really well," said Hannah. "Most of the water runs through it. It drains quickly, too. But the soil in my back garden drains really badly. It holds most of the water. What does drip through is really slow."

"Want to know why?" said Norman.

"No thank you," said Hannah. "I'll find out for myself."

Hannah got a book on gardening. She looked up soils.

What do you think She found out?

You may have a sandy soil, Hannah read. *Sandy soil is made up of big particles, and the water drains through it easily and quickly.*

"That sounds like my front garden," thought Hannah.

If you have a clay soil, the book continued, *then the soil is made of tiny particles. These hold the water and stop it draining away.*

"That's like my back garden!" thought Hannah. She read more.

The best soil is loam. Loam is a mixture of clay and sand that drains easily and supports growing plants well.

"But what should I do?" said Hannah.

What should Hannah do?

"What are you doing now?" Norman asked.

"I'm digging sand into the clay soil," said Hannah. "That way I will make it lighter and more like loam. It will drain better, of course, and my plants will grow well."

"Oh," said Norman. "You think you know everything."

"I do," said Hannah.

Scientific Enquiry

Test how well two soils drain

Use the planning board on Task Sheet 10 to help you set up an investigation to test how well two soils drain.

✻ Which soil drains best?

✻ How do you know? What evidence do you have?

✻ What difference does it make if you add sand to the soil that drains poorly?

✻ Why do you think that is?

YOU NEED:

soil samples from 2 different places

two funnels

set of scales

water

seconds timer

measuring jug

some plastic gloves for handling soil

Words to learn and use:
loam
sieve
soil profile
talcum powder

Checkpoint 1

The rock inspector

Bathrooms are full of rocks. Just think about the things in a bathroom - windows, tiles, taps, toilets, plastic bottles and talcum powder.

- What are all these made from?

- Draw a picture of a bathroom and label each thing in it to show what it's made from.

- Try to find out how rocks are used to make these bathroom things, too.

  - Pumice
  - Plastic shower curtains
  - Toothpaste

- Choose a different kind of room and try to identify more rocks in it.

Checkpoint 2

Wonder Soil

Look at this newspaper advert for Wonder Soil.

Why waste water?
Wonder Soil holds all the rain that falls on it **AND** all the water you pour on it.

Why waste space?
Wonder Soil is tightly packed with no air spaces. Lots more plants can grow in it!

Why waste money?

It's ONLY £9.99 for a bag and £14.99 for a giant bag.

- Fax or email The Wonder Soil Company. Tell them what you think of their product - and why.

Summary

Which of these do you know and which can you do?

- I know that you can use rocks for many different purposes.
- I know that you can sort rocks by how they look.
- I know that different rocks suit different jobs.
- I know that there is rock under you, wherever you are.
- I know that different types of rock make different types of soil.
- I know that you can separate particles of different sizes by sieving.
- I can find differences between rocks by testing.
- I can observe and compare rocks and soils.
- I can measure amounts of liquids and time.
- I can plan a fair test.

Complete your **Science Log** to show how well you know these and how well you can do them. Circle a face for each statement.